MADONNA MIA! IT'S FINALLY HERE!

MERDA!
The REAL Italian You Were Never Taught in School

How can you forget your Italian teacher's flustered face when you asked her all those words and phrases that she would never translate for you? How about when you and your fellow classmates searched in vain for the mildest expletives in your Italian-English dictionary? Did you ever wonder what the young men lining the streets of Rome were saying to the American women? or about those outrageous hand gestures that speak more than a thousand words? Here at last is a humorous, uncensored guide to the off-color colloquialisms that are so essential to a true understanding of everyday Italian. *Merda!* goes far beyond those prim and starchy lesson manuals to bring you the real Italian they'd never dare teach you in school: shocking idioms . . . hard-core curses . . . scatological words for body functions and body parts . . . pithy epithets for every nasty occasion . . . detailed descriptions of insulting hand gestures . . . and much more. Now you too can take on the Italian language in its most passionate form.

D0110318

Merda!

The REAL Italian You Were Never Taught in School

Roland Delicio

Illustrated by KIM WILSON EVERSZ

A PLUME BOOK

PLUME
Published by the Penguin Group
Penguin Books USA Inc., 375 Hudson Street,
New York, New York 10014, U.S.A.
Penguin Books Ltd, 27 Wrights Lane,
London W8 5TZ, England
Penguin Books Australia Ltd, Ringwood,
Victoria, Australia
Penguin Books Canada Ltd, 10 Alcorn Avenue,
Toronto, Ontario, Canada M4V 3B2
Penguin Books (N.Z.) Ltd, 182–190 Wairau Road,
Auckland 10, New Zealand

Penguin Books Ltd, Registered Offices:
Harmondsworth, Middlesex, England

First published by Plume, an imprint of Dutton Signet,
a division of Penguin Books USA Inc.

First Printing, November, 1993
10 9 8 7

Copyright © Roland Delicio, 1993
All rights reserved

Ⓟ REGISTERED TRADEMARK—MARCA REGISTRADA

LIBRARY OF CONGRESS CATALOGING-IN-PUBLICATION DATA:
Delicio, Roland.
    MERDA! : the real Italian you were never taught in school / by
 Roland Delicio ; illustrated by Kim Wilson Eversz.
      p.   cm.
    ISBN 0-452-27039-1
    1. Italian language—Slang.   2. Italian language—Obscene words.
 3. Italian language—Conversation and phrase books—English.
 I. Title.
 PC1961.D45   1993
 457'.09—dc20   93-7731
                                                        CIP

Printed in the United States of America
Set in Janson
Designed by Leonard Telesca

Without limiting the rights under copyright reserved above, no part of this publication
may be reproduced, stored in or introduced into a retrieval system, or transmitted, in any
form, or by any means (electronic, mechanical, photocopying, recording, or otherwise),
without the prior written permission of both the copyright owner and the above publisher
of this book.

BOOKS ARE AVAILABLE AT QUANTITY DISCOUNTS WHEN USED TO PROMOTE PRODUCTS OR
SERVICES. FOR INFORMATION PLEASE WRITE TO PREMIUM MARKETING DIVISION, PENGUIN BOOKS
USA INC., 375 HUDSON STREET, NEW YORK, NEW YORK 10014.

FOR

Amelia, the source
Anita, who made it possible
Merendolina, who supplied some of the
     ammunition
and to the memory of my Tuscan
     grandmother who, when I was a child,
     sang the following with a blend of
     insouciance and wicked innocence:

E con lo zigo zago, morettino vago
Me l'hai rotto l'ago, m'hai ferito il cuore
Mi farai morir, mi farai morir
Dalla passione mi sento svenir.

None of the above, however, is any way
responsible for the bawdy excesses of this
terrible little book. I—the only begetter of
this offense to the common good—await the
punishment due me. Mea culpa! That
punishment—inevitably—will be flaming
and Faustian.

Contents

Contents

Preface

Italians are friendly, right? Smiling Latins who will give you everything they have, including their mellifluous language. You couldn't possibly imagine the Italian language—whose very grocery lists sound like an aria by Puccini—being capable of producing the vilest obscenities, right? Or could you?

You are in Italy and an old man smiles and says to you, "*Americani, pezzi di merda!*" Of course, you smile graciously. The old *paisano* is praising Americans and apple pie. Wrong. He has just told you—in the most unrestrained slang—that Americans are pieces of shit.

You are an attractive young lady traveling alone in Florence and an abnormally handsome hunk you met in the Uffizi is sitting across from you at a cozy table in the Piazza della Signoria, and he says to you soulfully, "*Come vorrei chiavare con te stasera.*" You are delighted. He looks like the beautiful Italian in Hawthorne's novel whose title you can't remember. You have two degrees in literature and a bad memory, but you just *love* all things Italian. Obviously, he wants to discuss the iconography in Botticelli's paintings with you. Wrong. He

Preface

has just bluntly said, albeit in a poetic tone of voice reminiscent of Marcello Mastroianni, that he wants to fuck you tonight.

You are walking down a street in Venice (yes, there *are* streets in Venice) with your wife, Myrtle, who has gone recklessly to fat, when you are stopped by a delicate old lady Myrtle has just bumped into. *"Quella donna ha un culo pericoloso,"* says the frail lady benignly as she looks at Myrtle's body like an appraiser. You have heard that Italians appreciate "buxom" women, so you accept what must be a compliment. Wrong. The old lady has just said, as bluntly and explicitly as the aforementioned young satyr in the piazza, "That woman's ass is dangerous."

You are back in the United States visiting Greenwich Village in New York City, with its still-vibrant Italian-American population. You are with your girlfriend and happen to look at a guy in a perfectly casual way. *"Finocchio, stronzo!"* snaps the young man in smiling contempt. You nod pleasantly and answer *grazie*, the only word you remember from that two-week Perillo tour of Italy you and Sheila took. The guy said something gracious, did he not? Wrong. He called you a faggot and a turd.

You continue walking. Somewhere in Little Italy, two very old Italian ladies seem to be having a disagreement. *"Figlia di puttana!"* shouts the first. *"Vaffanculo!"* answers her snarling antagonist vehemently. *"Cafona!"* howls the first. *"Avanzo di galera!"* rages the second. *"Tuo padre era un rotto in culo!"* shrieks the first triumphantly. Fortunately, their respective family members break up the slight disagreement. The women are in their eighties and fragile. If their exchange had had subtitles, you would have read: Daughter of a bitch! Go fuck yourself! Peasant! Jailbird! Your father took it up the ass!

Mellifluous Italian? Puccini? Wrong.

Now you are blushing slightly and quicky take off with Sheila in tow. You seem to remember some of the words exchanged by the two old crones. Dave Manfredi and Joe

Preface

Anzalone, buddies on the team back at old Syracuse High, used to shout words (maybe in mutilated form) that sounded very much like these at each other in the locker room after those chilly autumn games. Even the guys who weren't Italian had learned them and kicked them around in these mutilated versions. But you were never quite sure exactly what they really did mean. Now you wish you hadn't been frightened by foreign languages in high school and college. But even if you had studied Italian, you would not have learned what you will from this compact introduction to Italian slang.

Don't despair. It's not too late. This little book, whether you read it for pleasure and enlightenment, or whether you take it with you as a traveling companion, can help you immeasurably.

Remember, what follows is the *real* Italian that no one is ever taught in school.

In the examples above, some of the operative words were: *merda*, *chiavare*, *culo*, *finocchio*, *stronzo*, *puttana*, *cafona*. In English: shit, to fuck, ass, faggot, turd, whore, peasant. Wouldn't it have been convenient to know this? *Ma naturalmente!* Would your teacher have included them in his daily vocabulary drill? *Ma assolutamente no!*

As one can see, slang in any language doesn't pull any punches. But isn't self-defense about knowing how to punch back? And really that's all we want to do—help you to give back what you get, or at least to know whether you are being complimented or insulted in Italian.

Senza dubbio, we are all persons of great breeding and try to avoid the scatalogical at all costs. We assiduously unfurl the banners of good taste. The decision is entirely one's own. We can opt to walk away with dignity and *fare da sordo* (pretend to be deaf), or we can rebut in kind.

What follows, then, in the simplest format, is a guide to those Italian words both proper and improper, singly and in convenient phrases and sentences, with a guide to their pronunciation, some basic grammar, and a few other practical aids that should admit you—if only tentatively—into that august fraternity whose legendary members include Boccaccio, Petrarca, and Signor Dante Alighieri himself.

Buona fortuna!

A Note on Dialects

When I mentioned to an Italian friend of mine that I had been asked to write a short introduction to Italian slang for English readers, he answered without hesitation: "Impossible! You would have to include all the dialects." Of course, he was right.

I, however, was equally adamant in my belief that the book would have to be confined to standard Italian. A dictionary of Italian slang that included all the dialects would be—of necessity—a monumental work of scholarship, and scholarship is certainly not what the casual English reader wants at this point. It is best, therefore, to placate those Italians and Italian-Americans who may peruse these pages and come away angry. Where are those funny, dirty words my grandfather used to shout at me when I misbehaved? Why do the words in this book look and sound only a little like them, and why are they spelled the way they are?

Because they are written and to be pronounced in standard Italian, I am obliged to respond. I don't wish to ignore the racy expletives (many exclusive to a particular dialect and having nothing at all to do with standard Italian) of Nonno Francesco from Calabria, or Nonno Innocente from Piemonte, or Nonno Nicola from Puglia, or Nonno Gualtiero from the Veneto, or Nonno Turiddu from Sicilia, but standard Italian is the Italian derived from Dante and is understood by all Italians with some education from Mount Etna to the Alps. Dialects are still spoken throughout Italy, but most Italians are bilingually Italian—that is, they switch from dialect to standard Italian as suits the occasion.

So, gentle reader, do not feel slighted.

A Note on Translation

The glossary at the end of this book is far from complete, but it attempts to include most of the words used in the text and some others. Italian taboo words are underlined in the text and the glossary (the English ones are obvious) so that you will be aware of the degree of vulgarity or rudeness inherent in them. Wherever possible, I have tried to supply the closest English slang equivalent, but unfortunately it's hard to be completely consistent. But what *is* slang nowadays? The media now overwhelm us with language so explicit that it is difficult to decide exactly what can or cannot be uttered in front of Grandma and the kids. Furthermore, slang is a cultural phenomenon. What seems natural to Italians or the French may seem offensive to Anglo-Saxons. The very euphony of Italian may make a taboo word sound like poetry. The brutal sibilance of the Anglo-Saxon *shit* is quite another thing when placed beside the Italian *merda*. Do you see what I mean? The mellifluous can really be a trap. In any case, note carefully all underlined words if you are overwrought about creating bad impressions. But remember, *Merda!* is, after all, an introduction to *The Real Italian You Were Never Taught in School*, not the Italian of diplomatic protocol.

Ed adesso, avanti!

1
Basics, Bastards, and Naughty Nuances

This book is mainly an introduction to Italian slang, not a comprehensive phrase book for travelers. If you do take it with you to Italy, it probably will be one of several language guides in your possession. The book will supply you with the profane. The others should supply the marginally sacred. Not, of course, that *Merda!* overlooks polite ways of being scurrilous. What follows are some of the basic words—both naughty and nice—that most of us need in a new language, except that here most will be given with impolite examples in order to introduce you quickly to X-rated vocabulary. In traveling, polite terms are essential. We do meet people. We do need rest rooms. We may need a policeman in a hurry, or the American consul, or a drink, or directions, or medical attention, or God knows what. The zesty words should be held in reserve for those particular occasions when patience wears thin. The Italian word *slancio* suggests throwing yourself into something, doing something with vigor. You must have *slancio* when confronting both life and language. The Italian language is an aggressive music. When you speak its rowdier epithets, imagine yourself one of your favorite operatic villains—an unctuous Baron Scarpia, a mordant Iago, a smiling, insidious Mephistopheles. If pronunciation is a concern, consult the appropriate chapter. Otherwise—*avanti!*

People

a man	un uomo
a pimp	un ruffiano
a big-bellied slob	un buzzone
a woman	una donna
a whore, a hooker	una puttana
a cheap cunt	una bagascia, una spuderata
a son	un figlio
a son of a bitch	un figlio di puttana
an ugly kid	un aborto (literally an abortion)
a husband	un marito
a cuckold	un cornuto
a wife	una moglie
a daughter	una figlia
a friend	un amico, una amica
a piece of ass	una fica pronta (literally, a ready cunt)

2

Merda!

a well-hung guy	uno ben armato
a big-breasted babe	una poppona
a girl	una ragazza
a sexually insatiable girl	<u>un assatanata</u>
a boy	un ragazzo, un giovanotto
an effeminate boy	<u>un finocchino</u>
parents	i genitori
a grandmother	una nonna

Merda!

a bimbo	**una pazzarella**
a hunk	**uno forte e ben armato**
a grandfather	**un nonno**
dad	**papa, babbo**
mom	**mamma, mammina**
a family	**una famiglia**
a mother-in-law	**una suocera**
a father-in-law	**un suocero**
a buddy	**un compagno, un amico caro**
an old woman	**una vecchia**
an old man	**un vecchio**
a dyke	**una finocchia**
a faggot	**un finocchio, un frocio**
a brother	**un fratello** (beware—this also means the penis)
a sister	**una sorella** (beware—this also means the vulva)
a shit	**un merdoso, una merdosa**

an asskisser	**un leccaculo, una leccaculo**
a sleaze	**un farabutto**
a drunkard	**un briacone, una briacona**
a stinker	**un vigliacco, un puzzolente**
a sucker, a gullible one	**un fesso, una fessa** (beware—in southern dialects **la fessa** means the vulva)
a tart	**una troia**
a virgin	**una vergine**
a shithead	**un testa di merda**
a slob	**un sporcaccione**
a phony	**un imbroglione, un falso**
a good lay	**una puttana pronta** (literally, a whore who's ready for action)
a big mouth, a gossip	**un boccalone, una boccalona** (literally, an enormous mouth)
a jerk	**un bischero** (beware —this also means the penis)

a gangster	un malvivente, un mafioso
a dingbat	un stonato, una stonata
a ballbuster	<u>un rompacoglioni, una rompacoglioni</u>

Let's Feast on Some Erotic Word Couplings

A noun alone is a desolate thing: breasts, ass, lips. An adjective alone is equally lonely: magnificent, voluptuous, hot. Link them and language lives: magnificent breasts, voluptuous ass, hot lips. Now let's put some modifiers to work in Italian and observe how the blossoms of language open up to our linguistic importunities.

a wife who sleeps around	una moglie <u>sgualdrina</u>
a sexy daughter	una figlia <u>puttanesca</u>
a fellating friend	un amico che fa <u>pompini</u>
a gal who spreads her legs	<u>un amica che apre le gambe</u>
a boy who jerks off	un ragazzo che si <u>frega</u>
stupid parents	genitori strulli, stupidi
a senile grandmother	una nonna bisbetica

a ditzy mom	una mamma sbalordita
a shit of a mother-in-law	una <u>merda</u> d'una suocera
a turd of a father-in-law	un <u>stronzo</u> d'un suocero
a dirty old woman	una vecchia <u>puzzolente</u>
an old man who farts	un vecchio <u>scureggione</u>
a country of cuckolds	un paese di cornuti
a toilet for slobs	un cesso per <u>fetenti</u>
to wash one's ass	<u>lavarsi il culo</u>
the fucking police	quei <u>vaffanculi</u> della polizia

Places

a city	una città
a country	un paese
a street	una via, una strada
customs	la dogana
the airport	l'aeroporto
a square	una piazza
a brothel	un bordello, una casa di tolleranza
any shabby, dirty place	<u>un merdaio</u>
a shack	una baracca

Travel, Emergencies, Personal Needs, and Some Heartbreaking Imprecations

a rest room, a toilet	un gabinetto, un cesso, un licito
a bath (in a tub)	un bagno nella vasca
a shower	una doccia
water	acqua
damn the cold water	maledetta l'acqua fredda
clean	pulito
to wash	lavare
unclean	sporco
as filthy as pigs	sporco come maiali
a condom	un condom, un preservativo
a toothbrush	uno spazzolino da denti
private	privato
do not enter	vietato entrare
to sleep	dormire
to sleep late	dormire tardi
to the left	alla sinistra

to the right	alla destra
lost between the legs	<u>perduto fra le gambe</u>
to find	trovare
an erection	<u>un cazzo ritto</u>
departure	la partenza
arrival	l'arrivo
at what time?	a che ora?
direction	la direzione
to be lost	essere perduto, essere perduta
I'm lost	sono perduto, sono perduta
where?	dove?
where is?	dov'é?
the police	la polizia
a doctor	un dottore, un medico
to be sick	essere malato, essere malata
to be sick of this fucking country	<u>essere stanco di questo vaffanculo d'un paese</u>
pain	il dolore
help!	aiuto!

Merda!

I need	cerco, ho bisogno di
I need a woman (man)	ho bisogno d'una donna (d'un uomo)
a tourist	un turista
that stupid fucking tourist	<u>quel vaffanculo d'un turista</u>
I'm an American tourist	sono un turista americano
I don't feel well	non mi sento bene
I'm thirsty	ho sete
I need a doctor	ho bisogno d'un medico
I'm looking for my hotel	cerco il mio albergo
I need a dentist	ho bisogno d'un dentista
fire	fuoco
hunger	fame
what a fucking world!	<u>mondo boia! mondo cane!</u>

Let's Abuse Our Body Parts

No, not *that* kind of abuse. We are not regressing to child-hood. We are examining that hilarious irony—the allusion to our private parts when uttering the most salacious insults. Why irony? Because these sacred organs of love and procrea-

11

tion become a double-edged sword. Dumb prick! Cunt! We do it in English, and it is equally valid in Italian. Man, as the great ones have told us, is somewhat of an enigma. He will profane the sacred with reckless eloquence, but too often he cannot speak two sentences grammatically or with style. The English *cunt* and *prick* are universal taboo words, but used as personal insults they lose some of their gutter credentials and connote degrees of stupidity and incompetence. Strange, isn't it, that we think so little of our genitalia?

Well, it is all the same in Italian. *Cazzo* and *fica* are taboo words, but many a well-bred and dignified Italian will not hesitate to call some clumsy oaf tripped up in some egregious *faux pas* a *cazzo* or *cazzone*. The Italian *fica*, however, is something else. It cannot be used to indicate abject stupidity or clumsiness the way *cazzo* does. Yes, in English you will occasionally hear one man call another a cunt, but this is comically impossible in Italian. You cannot call an Italian man *una fica* and expect not to endanger the symmetry of your teeth. In Tuscany alone, however, might you get away with calling

a man who is a bit too delicate or too fastidious or too silly
un ficone or *un fichino*, but nowhere else. *Fico* is altogether
another word. It means *fig*. Note that *cazzo* and *coglione* both
indicate a degree of stupidity and are interchangeable.

the head	**la testa**
the eye	**l'occhio**
the nose	**il naso**
the mouth	**la bocca**
the neck	**il collo**
the back	**la schiena**
the breasts	**le poppe**, i petti, **le cioccie**
the stomach	**lo stomaco**
the cunt	**la fica, la potta**
the prick	**il cazzo, la minchia, i coglioni**
the ass	**il culo**
the balls	**le palle, i coglioni**
the buttocks	**le chiappe, le mele**
the legs	**le gambe**
the feet	**i piedi**

Some Useful Phrases

a fool, a nerd, a dummy, a jerk, a moron, an asshole	una testa di cazzo
a dirty whore, a filthy slut	una puttana lercia, una bagascia, una fica di strada
a big-breasted tramp	una poppona sgualdrina
an easy lay, a piece of ass	una fica pronta, una fica stretta
a dummy, a first-class asshole	un cazzo, un cazzone, un cazzaccio, un coglione, un coglionaccio di prima classe
a big erection, a cock that's ready, willing, and able	un gran cazzo ritto, un bel cazzo pulito e pronto (literally, a beautiful cock that's clean and ready)
a worn-out old whore	una vecchia fica rotta
a deep-throated cocksucker	una pompinaia
a cuntlapper par excellence	un pompinaio di classe
a hot pussy	una fica di fiamme

Merda!

play with yourself! jerk off!   **va a farti una fregata!**

that big-assed sleaze   **quella culona troia**

Now It's Time to Try Your Hand at Some Practical Swearing

1. **Vorrei chiavare quella bella fica.**
2. **Quel cazzone non sa il davanti dal dietro.**
3. **Mio figlio è il più gran coglione della sua classe.**
4. **Quella puttana è la signorina Coscieaperte del quartiere.**
5. **Le parolacce italiane veramente hanno coglioni.**

1. I'd like to fuck that hot pussy.
2. That asshole doesn't know front from back.
3. My son is the biggest idiot in his class.
4. That slut is Miss Openthighs of the neighborhood.
5. Italian slang really has balls.

A Note on Pronunciation

There is a short guide to pronunciation in the next chapter. You don't have to read it. But if you do read it, then you will probably speak what you choose to speak in Italian with greater clarity and precision, not to say conviction. Italian vowels must be respected. They must never open up sloppily as they do in English. Consonants present no special problem. But double consonants and trilled *r*'s, if not rattled and rolled, will weaken Italian invective, presuming that you are brave enough to attempt the vituperative in Italian. In producing the curse, as in all verbal communication, diction is paramount.

When a Woody Allen character was asked why he was such a great lover, his answer was that he practiced when he was alone. Solitary practice is also a helpful approach in acquiring a facility with Italian slang. Of course, practice with another person might prove invaluable and mutually enlightening, particularly if that other person is a native Italian. But beware—words can easily become aphrodisiacs.

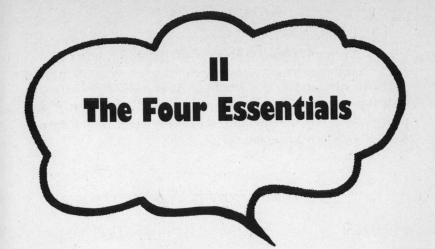

II
The Four Essentials

Sine Qua Non, or What
You Cannot Do Without

A cannon without ammunition is useless. And so it is with slang. If slang is to supply powerful vitriolic fusillades, then ammunition must always be at hand. Four words in Italian are the most powerful. These four words are succinct. They will penetrate any target. They encapsulate, in their singular and rich connotations, delicious vituperation. Why else is one of them the title of this book?

Above all, do not let any Italian-American who knows a few words in a dialect mislead you into thinking that they are either misspelled or incorrect. You will say them proudly in the Italian of Dante—in Tuscan—and later, if you are so inclined, you might spend a few seconds on pronunciation.

First, That *Merda* Word

Merda means shit. It is impolite. It is rude. It is earthy. It is unequivocally taboo. But if used sparingly and with appropriate contextual imagination, its two-syllable simplicity can assume Homeric resonances.

This Is How It Works

a shithead	una testa di merda
a shitface	una faccia di merda
a shit (foul) mouth	una bocca di merda
a shitty ass	un culo di merda
a shitty dinner	un pranzo di merda
a mountain of shit	una montagna di merda
a shit among shits	una merda fra merde
shit for shit	merda per merda
a catastrophic failure	finire in merda (literally, to end in shit)

Try These for Additional Prurient Practice

1. Il mio marito è una testa di merda.
2. Parigi lo trovata una montagna di merda.

3. Il nostro matrimonio andò a finire in merda.
4. Sono stanca della tua bocca di merda.
5. Sei proprio una faccia di merda.

1. My husband is a shithead.
2. Paris was just one mound of shit.
3. Our marriage ended in shit.
4. I'm sick of your foul mouth.
5. You really are one hell of a shitface.

Merda takes on spectacular heights of vituperation when suffixes are added. You remember suffixes from high school —those additions to words that alter meaning. *Love* becomes *lovable*. *Operate* becomes *operator*. *Fuck* becomes *fucker* or *fuckee*. Italian suffixes stretch the root word to truly offensive ends. Take note of how in the words *merdonaccio* and *merdonettaccio* multiple suffixes turn the already scurrilous into something even more dazzlingly scurrilous. O what a language is Italian! More material on suffixes is included in a later chapter. Note carefully the delightful changes in meaning.

shit	**la merda**
one reeking of shit	**un merdoso**
a dirty place, a place reeking of shit	**un merdaio**
a shitmonger, a sleaze, a fuck, a lowlife, one who figuratively traffics in shit	**un merdaiolo**
a low-down shit, an unclean person, a turd	**un merdaccio**

small quantities of shit (what an infant haphazardly produces)	<u>merdina</u>
a big shit	<u>una merdona</u>
a big, nasty shit	<u>un merdonaccio</u>
a small, cute shit	<u>un merdonetto</u>
a small, cute, but nasty shit	<u>un merdonettaccio</u>

Vaffanculo

Vaffanculo means go fuck yourself—among many other things. It is extremely impolite. It is more rude than *merda*. It is taboo but ubiquitous. It also connotes fuck you, fuck off, up your ass, go to hell, get off my case, go and take it up the ass, shit on you, get lost, shove it, sit on it, beat it, buzz off, and comparable angry dismissive slang terms of similar intensity. If you have heard no other Italian slang word, you may have heard this one, too often mispronounced in some dialect. Say it now with oratorical purity: *VAF FAN CU LO*. Embrace this term with solicitous possession. It can be a friend in need.

Sample phrases are really not necessary for this term. It is the ideal one-short-statement put-down any time you are deeply disgruntled and ready to let someone have it. Just take a deep breath and say: *Vaffanculo!*

Sentence Practice for *Merda* and *Vaffanculo*

1. **Quello ha un gran dono. Tutto che tocca finisce in merda.**
2. **Vaffanculo! Non sono la tua puttana!**

3. Sei il secondo merdoso del mondo. Il mio marito è il primo.
4. Ecco il mio vaffanculo d'un marito.
5. Non sei più una merda. Adesso sei un vero stronzo.
6. Fra noi tutto è finito. Vaffanculo!
7. Se la merda porta fortuna, dovrei essere la più ricca donna del mondo.
8. Fai l'amore come una macchina. Vaffanculo!
9. In una gara di merdosi, il primo premio deve a te.
10. Sei il più grande vaffanculo che ho mai conosciuto.

1. He's a talented guy. Everything he touches turns to shit.
2. Fuck off! I'm not your whore!
3. You're the world's second biggest shit; my husband is the first.
4. There goes my fuckoff of a husband.
5. You're no longer simply a shit. Now you're a full-fledged turd.
6. It's over between us. Fuck off!
7. If shit brings good luck, then I should be the world's richest woman.
8. You make love like a machine. Screw yourself!
9. In a contest of shits, you'd get the first prize.
10. You're the biggest asshole I've ever known.

Cafone

Cafone can be used safely and demurely by everyone. It is not exactly polite, but it certainly is not taboo. You will hear it in the most elegant drawing rooms, in the convent, in *recherché* latitudes, in those hallowed corridors where heads of state loiter, and at the driest scholarly gatherings. A standard Italian dictionary will define *cafone* as a peasant, a crude person, a villain, an uneducated person. How trippingly on the tongue you utter it will determine its impact. Say it with gusto and you can trounce the rabble. Say it flaccidly and you will be as effective as a moribund wind machine. The circumspect multitude that eschews "common" talk should feel relatively safe using it (if these virginal types can ever feel safe with anything). Its connotations are infinite. If you want to react verbally to any of the following, use it without trepidation, but produce it with panache: bad manners, boorishness, vulgarity, bad taste (don't shake your gory locks at this writer), crudeness, coarseness, impertinence, stubbornness, insolence, arrogance, insensitivity, crassness, stupidity, or, in other words, as the linguistically careless mumble nowadays—whatever.

Some Choice Morsels

a stupid jerk	**un cazzone cafone**
a first-class asshole	**un cafone di prima classe**
a son of an ignorant clod	**un figlio d'un cafone**
a crude slob	**un cafone rozzo**
a tasteless blob	**un cafone sciocco**
an ill-mannered fool	**un cafone maleducato**
an officious ass	**un cafone impertinente**
a tasteless crud	**un cafone senza gusto**
a disgusting boor	**un cafone ripugnante**

Spring One of These on Your Favorite
Cafone, Cafona, or Cafoni

1. Appartieni alla famiglia reale dei cafoni.
2. Sei il figlio cafone di genitori cafoni.
3. Il tuo cafonismo non ha limiti.
4. Adossi il cafonismo come un mantello.
5. Il puzzo del tuo cafonismo avvelena l'aria.

1. You belong to the royal family of slobs.
2. You are the uncouth son of uncouth parents.
3. Your grossness knows no bounds.
4. You wear stupidity like a mantle.
5. The stench of your ignorance poisons the air.

Antipatico

Antipatico is a second mild expletive that can be used safely by the stiff-upper-lipped, as well as by those looser of lip. It is not quite as cutting as *cafone*, but it is suitably derogatory. Both *cafone* and *antipatico* are convenient euphemisms for Italians who want to express displeasure without slumming in the spiky world of slang. It means the opposite of *simpatico*, a word you probably knew even before you opened this book. *Antipatico* denotes something or someone you have an instinctive aversion to for any number of reasons. It is not quite as operatic as *cafone*, but it does connote what is annoying, boring, dull, insipid, tiresome, predictable, déjà vu, fatuous, otiose, and flat.

Some Palpable Phrases

to be a real drag	fare l'antipatico
you're drab, dull, boring	sei antipatico, sei antipatica
a tiresome joke	una barzelletta antipatica
a dreary hotel	un albergo antipatico
a boring lover	un amante antipatico, una amante antipatica
a dull city	una città antipatica
an annoying man	un uomo antipatico
a disappointing vacation	una vacanza antipatica
dreary people	persone antipatiche

And Some Sentences That Might Come in Handy

1. Tuoi baci antipatici sono sciocchi come una fava.
2. E meglio che a letto non fai l'antipaticone!
3. Sei antipatico quando dormi e quando sei sveglio.
4. Moglie antipatica, chiavata antipatica.
5. La morte è l'unica cura per il vero antipatico.

1. Your kisses are as boring and bland as a bean.
2. Bed with you had better not be dullsville!

24

3. You're as tedious asleep as you are awake.
4. Dull wife, dull fucking.
5. Death is the only cure for the truly dull.

If you learn nothing else, these last two words—*cafone* and *antipatico*—can be your best friends on your next trip to Italy,

or communicating in Italian with Italians anywhere. *Merda* and *vaffanculo*, as pointed out, must be used with great circumspection. They are universal, popular obscenities, but they are irrefutably taboo. Use them at your own risk. They may raise more than eyebrows; they may raise fists.

A Very Short Guide to Pronunciation to Really Get It Right

You now have the rudiments of Italian slang. Confidence will grow quickly as you savor the organ meats of language. *Ris de veau* will always have its place in the refined parameters of gustatory gastroporn, but there are times when tripe and tripe alone seduces the stomach with its chewy and aromatic importunities. Slang is like tripe. Now let's be sure we pronounce these new words with the boisterous accuracy that will do them justice, because if you care to insult someone in Italian and you pronounce *merda* as the English *murder*, you will provoke laughter instead of anger. Fractured standard Italian is a linguistic comedy of errors to be scrupulously avoided—and with slang we must be equally fastidious.

If you have studied a Romance language, you are ahead of the game. Better yet, if you speak even a little French, Spanish, or Japanese, join the privileged. If you don't—well, it just doesn't matter a fiddler's fancy. Italian vowels are pronounced, in most cases, as they are in those languages. They are short—not oozed out like lava. Italian vowels do not echo and spread open like the sonics in a bad dream.

A is pronounced as the first *o* in English *bottom*, as in *bastardo* (bastard). *E* as the short *e* in *let*, as in *stronzetto* (little turd). *I* as the *e* in *me*, as in *finocchio* (faggot). *O* as English *ah*, but only with your lips shaped for *o* (Don't get hurt!), as in *fotto* (I fuck). *U* as the double *o* in *moo*, as in *culo* (ass). Say these for practice: *il cazzo* (the prick), *un leccaculo* (an ass kisser), *la minchia* (the cock), *il cornuto* (the cuckold), *la puttana* (the whore).

Consonants are the whores of language. They do what they are told in any language, but note the following. *C* and *g* before *e* or *i* are pronounced as *ch* in *chill* and *g* in *general*. *C* and *g* have a hard sound if followed by *a*, *o*, or *h*. We say *chianti* (kee-ahn-tee), not *shianti*. H is always silent. Double consonants must be pronounced with double emphasis, as in *palle* (balls) and *mille* (a thousand). If you do not give double consonants particular force, there will be little difference between *fica* (cunt) and *ficca* (he inserts). *Gli* is pronounced like *lli* in million, and *gn* is pronounced like *ni* in *onion*. *R* must be trilled with exaggerated vehemence. That's it, simplified.

Some End-of-Chapter Sentences to Gauge Our Progress

1. Brutto buzzone, figlio d'una troia, non mi toccare il culo!
2. C'è posto nel tuo culo lurido per due cazzi duri.
3. Un francese lo prende in bocca, un inglese lo prende in culo.
4. Un marito è ciondolo conosciuto, un amante ti chiava per novità.
5. Mentre studiavo i miei vocali, una cosa dura m'entrò in bocca.

1. Get your hands off my ass, you fat-bellied son-of-a-bitch!
2. There's room in that filthy asshole of yours for two hard cocks.
3. A Frenchman takes it in the mouth, and an Englishman takes it up the ass.
4. A husband's dong is a familiar thing; a lover screws you for the hell of it.
5. While practicing my vowels, something hard found its way into my mouth.

III
Let's Be Creative

Creative Vituperation

Tourists are sitting ducks. They are ready targets for the locals, who often resent their presence. And what these testy locals utter under their breaths and out loud at the tourist is often choice and colorfully reprehensible.

We are in a restaurant in Milan, and even though it does not appear to be Chinese, things are evolving in a distinctly sweet and sour fashion. A reasonably polite but linguistically insecure tourist (this could be you) is being abused by an Italian waiter. The tourist is hungry and the waiter is underpaid, tired, and disgruntled. The tourist has read his copy of *Merda!* carefully on the flight over, but he hopes he will never have to resort to most of the words and phrases in the book. He has carefully reviewed the following terms relating to dining out and is ready to use them, albeit with some shyness.

a restaurant   **un ristorante**

an informal, inexpensive restaurant   **una trattoria**

Merda!

to reserve	**prenotare**
a table	**una tavola**
smoking	**fumando**
nonsmoking	**non fumando**
the menu	**il menu**
the appetizer	**l'antipasto**
the entree	**il primo piatto**
the dessert	**il dolce**
the salad	**l'insalata**
wine	**vino**
red wine	**vino rosso**
white wine	**vino bianco**
the check	**il conto**

The tourist is shown to a table, and a surly Italian waiter with a large nose, garlic breath, and an aggressive pugnacity approaches.

IL CAMERIERE:	Ciao, pappone.
IL TURISTA:	Volere menu, per favore.
IL CAMERIERE:	Volere quello che ho in mezzo alle gambe?
IL TURISTA:	Volere porco.
IL CAMERIERE:	Qui non si serve porco, si serve i porci.

IL TURISTA:	Prima volere pasta.
IL CAMERIERE:	Prima volere un cazzo in culo, finocchio americano!
IL TURISTA:	(blushing at words he begins to recognize) Per favore, mangiare.
IL CAMERIERE:	Per favore, mangiare questo!
IL TURISTA:	(getting angrier) Non mi piacere la tua lingua, signore.
IL CAMERIERE:	Se non vi piacere la lingua mia, frocio, andate a vaffanculo.
IL TURISTA:	(losing his temper) Lei vaffanculo, signore, e sua moglie e sua madre. Lei essere cafone stronzo. Io non mangiare in questo merdaio! Vaffanculo!
IL CAMERIERE:	Vaffanculo!

The English Version

WAITER:	Welcome, face-stuffer.
TOURIST:	I'd like a menu, please.
WAITER:	You'd like what I have between my legs?
TOURIST:	I want some pork.
WAITER:	We don't serve pork here, but we do serve pigs.
TOURIST:	First, I want some pasta.
WAITER:	First, you want my cock up your ass, you American faggot!
TOURIST:	Please, I want to eat.
WAITER:	Please, eat this!

Merda!

TOURIST: I don't like your language, sir.

WAITER: If you don't like my language, faggot, then fuck off!

TOURIST: You, sir, go fuck yourself—and your wife and your mother. You are a common turd! I'm not going to eat in this shithouse. Fuck you!

WAITER: Fuck you!

The tourist was goaded and finally resorted to slang. Doesn't this prove that there are moments when profanity might benefit from creative manipulation? As you can see, if your vituperation becomes an extension of yourself (the style is the man), then you will never find yourself humiliated as was the tourist in our sad little minidrama. Some preparation is therefore called for.

As in English, the scurrility of your raunchy put-downs depends upon the fertility of your imagination. The grotesque in life or language is merely the inventive manipulation of incongruities. And now that you have the basics, there is no reason why *you* shouldn't be able to manipulate and improve upon the horrors that follow. Onward! There is no turning back. Whether immersed in blood as was that miscreant the Thane of Cawdor, or in fecal matter as we are in danger of becoming, we must to the fight go valorously.

Tua faccia è un merdaio!
Your face is a shithouse!

Puzzi come un stronzo di cane!
You reek of dog shit!

Tua madre si da per niente!
Your mother gives it away!

33

Sei più marcio del putrido!
You make garbage smell sweet!

Pisciati in bocca!
Piss in your mouth!

Ti voglio chiavare a morte!
I want to fuck you to death!

Ciao, cara, fammi un bel pompino!
Blow me, babe!

Ti venisse un canchero secco nel culo!
May you drop dead of a desiccated cancer of the asshole!

Tuo padre è un finocchio rottinculo!
Your old man's a faggot who takes it up the ass!

Tua nonna ha dato nascita a una puttana!
Your grandmother gave birth to a cheap whore!

Morirai in merda dove ne hai vissuto!
You have lived and you will die in shit!

La tua bocca fu creata per fare pompini!
Your mouth was made to suck cock!

Buttati in un mare pieno di merda come te!
Why don't you throw yourself into an ocean that's as full of shit as you are!

As you can see, the possibilities are limitless. The thunder of hurled epithets fills the air. Lightning may conceivably strike twice. And please—pronounce those vowels with the stingy meanness of the anal retentive.

Pimps and Whores

What came first, the pimp or the whore? We will put that philosophical conundrum aside for the time being. All languages utilize the oldest profession as a way of verbally assaulting people who may deserve it. It lends itself to colorful analogies. Often it is easy to go beyond the merely colorful to the flamboyant. Italian is as rich as any other language in this usage. If you don't know by now, an Italian word for whore is *puttana*, and an Italian word for pimp is *ruffiano*. Let's see how we can use them singly and then in devilishly clever original combinations. Please bear with me if I occasionally repeat bits and pieces from other chapters. Redundancy is the refuge of every shy pornographer. But beware—this is PG country again. As the Florentine with the heroic nose warned:

Roland Delicio

Per me si va nella città dolente (Through me, you go into the city of pain).

Sei una puttana!
You are a whore!

Sei un ruffiano!
You are a pimp!

Sei una vecchia puttana!
You're an old whore!

Sei un ruffiano fetente!
You're a filthy pimp!

Sei una puttana di strada!
You're a streetwalking whore!

Sei un ruffiano impotente!
You're an impotent pimp!

Sei una puttanaccia!
You're a lousy whore!

Sei una puttanona!
You're a big whore!

Sei un ruffiano spuderato!
You're a sleazy pimp!

Sei un ruffiano senza coglioni!
You're a pimp without balls!

Sei una puttana senza clienti!
You're a whore without clients!

Sei un ruffiano per vacche e scimmie!
You're a pimp for cows and monkeys!

Sei una puttana con fica rotta!
You're an old whore with a busted twat!

Merda!

Sei un ruffiano travestito!
You're a pimp in drag!

Sei una puttana merdosa!
You're a shithouse whore!

Sei un ruffiano leccacazzi!
You're a cocksucking pimp!

Fai la ruffiana per il tuo ruffiano finocchio!
You're whoring for that faggot pimp of yours!

Sei la regina puttana della merda!
You're the queen shit of whores!

Sei un ruffiano che mangia merda!
You're a shit-eating pimp!

Once again, those of you who would like to avoid the risk of uttering complete sentences in a foreign language and who like the poetic brevity of the one-word put-down need only say *Puttana!* or *Ruffiano!* You will have made your point. Do you remember the word *slancio*? If you do, then those Italian buds previously mentioned (of your newly discovered Italian invective) should soon blossom into Venus flytraps.

Mafioso: Or the Shortest Chapter Ever Written

Are Italians proud of the Mafia? Are we proud of Charles Keating (remember him?) and the S & L scandal? Like it or not, the word *mafioso* is used as a handy Italian insult when describing an assortment of lowlifes, and it is heard more and more often in English-speaking countries as well.

For the curious: the word *mafia* comes from the Arabic *mahjas*, meaning to boast. Doesn't that say it all? Back in the nineteenth century, a secret society now universally known as the Mafia was founded. Intimidation, extortion, and murder were its prime activities. Things have merely intensified as it subsequently spread to other countries.

When does an Italian call someone *un mafioso*? When he is furious with someone's flagrant immorality. If any action is morally offensive in a blatant way, the word *mafioso* will do to express your disdain. Its many synonyms are: thief, crook, embezzler, murderer, liar, exploiter, adulterer, jailbird, two-timer, junkie, slime, sleaze, scum, venture capitalist, journalist, parasite, wheeler-dealer, politician, doctor, lawyer, Indian chief, etc.

When *mafioso* is used in tandem with some of the other juicy tidbits made available in this pioneer work of Italian lexicography, a work that occasionally brings a blush even to the cheeks of its only begetter, it will encourage you to aspire to a height of linguistic scabrousness you may have thought inaccessible to you.

Revel in These Terse Blockbusters

Brutto cafone mafioso!
You ugly cutthroat shit!

Stronzo mafioso maledetto!
You goddamned bloody gangster!

Mafioso leccaculo!
You asskissing hoodlum!

Mafioso lercio rottinculo!
You dirty asskissing faggot of a thug!

Fottete, mafioso spuderato!
Fuck off, you sleazy hood!

Vaffanculo, mafioso merdoso!
Go fuck yourself, you underworld lump of shit!

Mafioso, figlio di puttana!
You fucking gangster son of a bitch!

Figlio d'una puttana mafiosa!
You fucking son of a Mafia whore!

Brutto puzzolente mafioso!
You lowlife sewer scumbag!

Mafioso finocchio rottinculo!
Up your faggot gangster ass!

Some End-of-Chapter Savories to
Further Check Our Progress

1. Quel mafioso farabutto vuol sposare mia figlia.
2. Il mafioso comincia in carne ma finisce in cemento.
3. Il mafioso è veramente un uomo di famiglia.
4. Per il mafioso la morte è un modo di fare.
5. Il mafioso preferisce scannare, non ballare.

1. That mafioso bum wants to marry my daughter.
2. A mafioso begins as flesh but ends as concrete.
3. Your average mafioso is really just a nice family man.
4. For the mafioso, death is a means to an end.
5. The mafioso prefers cutting throats to cutting a caper. (Literally, the mafioso prefers slitting throats to dancing.)

Merda!

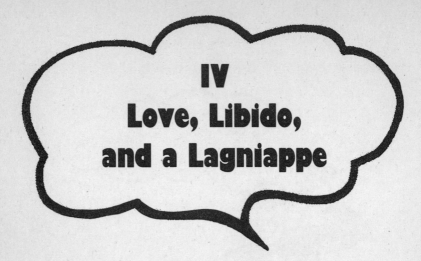

IV
Love, Libido,
and a Lagniappe

That's Amore: Even Educated Fleas
Do It

Let's Live Our Little Drama

We begin by eavesdropping on an Italian man trying to come on to an attractive American tourist. He doesn't speak English and she is doing her best to understand and speak Italian. His language is blunt. Her understanding is questionable.

Playlet: *Parlami D'Amore, Meez Smeeth*

GUIDO: Che petti hanno queste americane!

MEEZ SMEETH: Scusa.

GUIDO: Sono pazzo per te.

MEEZ SMEETH: Cosa volere?

Merda!

GUIDO:	Ti voglio inculare.
MEEZ SMEETH:	Non comprendere.
GUIDO:	Ti vorrei sbrodare.
MEEZ SMEETH:	In quale ristorante?
GUIDO:	Ti vorrei mangiare con un buon sugo.
MEEZ SMEETH:	Già avere mangiare in albergo, grazie.
GUIDO:	Ti vorrei fare un pompino.
MEEZ SMEETH:	Pompieri? Io non vedere fuoco.
GUIDO:	Pazza! Il fuoco è in mezzo alle mie gambe!
MEEZ SMEETH:	Ciao!
GUIDO:	Vado a casa a farmi una bella fregata.

The English Version

Playlet: *Speak to Me of Love, Meez Smeeth*

GUIDO:	American girls are really stacked!
MEEZ SMEETH:	Excuse me.
GUIDO:	I'm crazy about you.
MEEZ SMEETH:	What do you want?
GUIDO:	I want to sodomize you.
MEEZ SMEETH:	I don't understand.
GUIDO:	I want to make you come.
MEEZ SMEETH:	In which restaurant?

43

GUIDO:	I'd like to garnish you with a good sauce and eat you.
MEEZ SMEETH:	I already ate breakfast at the hotel, thank you.
GUIDO:	I'd like to go down on you.
MEEZ SMEETH:	Fireman? I don't see any fire.
GUIDO:	Idiot! The fire is between my legs.
MEEZ SMEETH:	See ya!
GUIDO:	I'm going home to jerk off.

Meez Smeeth's non sequitur is to be pardoned. She has confused *pompino* (a blow job) and *pompiere* (fireman), since both derive from *pompare* (to pump). And, unfortunately, the difference between *sbrodare* (to bring to sexual climax) and *brodo* (a soup stock) escapes her. Now, if she had read *Merda!* with greater assiduity, would this have happened?

The Italian Language of Love

Whether or not love is the final purpose of world history —the amen of the universe, or the requirement for uniting two currents, the tender and the sensual, or whether it is simply the rubbing of two intestines—is immaterial. Sexual love straddles the consciousness the way a hot jalapeño overwhelms the taste buds. It rides the heaving erotic waves of life with the gusto of a muscular surfer. We either accept this naturally or ignore it unnaturally. Some older people are now recommending abstinence to the young. Really! Have they forgotten?

It is rumored that Italians make a cult of love. Are they great lovers? There is one way to find out. Go to it! Casanova was Italian. He went to it. Let's examine some words and phrases to prove that Italians are never at a loss for words when it comes to *Amore*! Are you with us, Meez Smeeth? Recognize them when you hear them. Learn to use them yourself. It has been proven by assiduous researchers that foreplay is nine parts verbal and one part private.

I love you!	**Ti amo!**
I want you!	**Ti voglio!**
I need you!	**Ho bisogno di te!**
My passion! (sounds awful in English)	**Passione mia!**
Lover! My lover!	**Amore! Amore mio!**
I'm crazy about you!	**Sono pazzo per te!**
My soul! (not really very Anglo-Saxon)	**Anima mia!**
a bed	**un letto**
a position	**una posizione**
the first time	**la prima volta**
to make love	**far l'amore** (polite), **chiavare** (to fuck)
the tongue	**la lingua**
a hot tongue	**una lingua calda**
You're the only one!	**Sei l'unico! Sei l'unica!**
What a body!	**Che corpo!**
I would like	**vorrei**

Now Some That Are More or Less Impolite, Suggestive, and Explicit

Let's go to bed.	Andiamo a letto.
What tits, whoppers, knockers!	Che petti!
I'd like to put it . . .	voglio metterlo
How do you like it?	Come ti piace?
Suck it! Lick it!	Succhialo!
Swallow it!	Ingoialo!
Make me come!	Sbrodami!
a condom	un condom, un preservativo
to sodomize	inculare
cunnilingus, fellatio	fare un pompino
Do it!	Dai! (also heard at soccer games)
Squeeze it!	Strizzalo!
More!	Ancora!
Deeper!	Più profondo!
It hurts.	Fa male.
You're in.	Sei dentro.
It's so good!	E tanto buono!
It's marvelous!	E meraviglioso!

Merda!

Don't stop!	**Non fermare!**
I'm dying!	**Muoio!**
You're killing me!	**M'amazzi!**

Hyperbole, both polite and impolite, is to lovemaking in Italian as was the music of Richard Rodgers to the lyrics of Lorenz Hart. Romantic clichés must weight the air as humidity does a New York summer. Forget the fact that you are fastidious about language. So was Emily Dickinson. You must succumb gleefully to the coloratura madness of Lucia and her wimpy Edgardo as they keen libidinously in Donizetti's operatic violation of Sir Walter Scott's novel.

Restrained and Polite

I'll die without you!	**Morirò senza di te!**
I'll kill myself without you!	**Senza di te m'amazzo!**
I'll go crazy without you!	**M'impazzisco senza di te!**
The world is empty without you!	**Il mondo è vuoto senza di te!**
You're more beautiful than an angel!	**Sei più bella d'un angelo!**
I want to be with you forever!	**Voglio essere con te per eternità!**
I want you body and soul!	**Ti voglio anima e cuore!**

You're the Madonna (not the entertainer) of my life!	Sei la madonna della mia vita!
You're the most beautiful woman in the world!	Sei la più bella donna nel mondo!
There's no one like you!	Non ce nessuno come te!
Without you there's no sun up in the sky!	Senza di te non ce sole nel cielo!
Without you everything will end!	Senza di te tutto finirà!
Our love will last forever!	Il nostro amore non finirà mai!
I'll cut my throat if you leave me!	Mi scanno se me lasci!
I'll kill you if you leave me!	Se mi lasci t'amazzo!
You have the breasts of a goddess!	Hai i petti d'una dea.
Ours is the only love!	Il nostro è l'unico amore!

Now Let's Be Hyperbolic and Impolite and Sexually Explicit and Demonically Perverse

Yours is the biggest one I've ever seen!	Il tuo è il più grande che ho mai visto!
I'd like to eat you for breakfast!	Ti vorrei mangiare per colazione!

Merda!

I'm going to open your cute little lock with my big key!

Aprirò il tuo carino lucchettino colla mia grande chiave!

I want to walk into your cunt barefoot!

Voglio entrare la tua fica scalzo!

I'm going to ram it up your cunt and make it come out of your mouth!

Te lo ficcherò nella potta per fartelo uscire dalla bocca!

Fuck my face—it's no disgrace!

Chiavami in bocca, non è vergogna!

Boys and Girls Together

Guido and Meez Smeeth have been miraculously reincarnated as Eternal Man and Eternal Woman. He has finally lured her to his apartment after many Sambucas and heavier and heavier-lidded ogling. For the time being, she's not buying.

SHE: *You met him for the first time on the Piazza Indipendenza and he turns you on. But you don't want to seem too anxious. How would Glenn Close handle this?*

HE: *You know you're a great lover and you want her to benefit from this.*

SHE: *It's been a long week of musei and chiese. The last American tourist you had a drink with was a gay charmer from San Francisco's*

Merda!

*Castro district, and he was definitely not a convertible. You haven't
slept with a man in seven months and six days. Your facial hair will
probably grow in permanently if this goes on. But—damn it!—
you're a lady.*

Why will they be speaking in Italian? Because they are
reading this book. For the sake of romantic self-indulgence,
why don't we pretend that Guido is Dante Alighieri and Meez
Smeeth is his Beatrice. In Italy the fabulous is culturally in-
evitable. Only our Dante's desires go beyond spirituality.

DANTE: Mi piaci.

BEATRICE: Sei simpatico, ma . . .

DANTE: Anche tu sei simpatica. Hai un corpo
stupendo.

BEATRICE: Non sono una di quelle.

DANTE: Ti amo!

BEATRICE: Non mi toccare!

DANTE: Facciamelo!

BEATRICE: Hai la lingua calda. (Why is Meez
Smeeth/Beatrice's Italian so much better?
Because she can't stop reading her copy of
Merda!)

DANTE: Si allunga per te.

BEATRICE: Fermalo!

DANTE: Guarda com'è duro e grosso.

BEATRICE: Non mi far male.

DANTE: Come sei stretta.

BEATRICE: Non mi mordere la!

DANTE: Dai! Dai!

Merda!

BEATRICE: Amore! Sfondatemi! Mi fai impazzire! Mi hai empito!

DANTE: Vengo! Vengo!

BEATRICE: Sono una fontana!

DANTE: Che chiavata meravigliosa!

BEATRICE: Ti amo! Sposiamoci!

(And Just in Case You Still Need Translations . . .)

DANTE: I like you.

BEATRICE: You're a nice guy, but . . .

DANTE: You're a great gal, too. You're really built.

BEATRICE: I'm not one of those.

DANTE: I love you.

BEATRICE: Don't touch me!

DANTE: Let's do it!

BEATRICE: Your tongue's so hot.

DANTE: It's getting hard for you.

BEATRICE: Stop it!

DANTE: It's getting harder and longer.

BEATRICE: Don't hurt me.

DANTE: How tight you are.

BEATRICE: Don't bite me there!

DANTE: Do it! Do it!

BEATRICE: Lover! Shove it all the way in! You're driving me crazy! You've filled me to the brim!

DANTE:	I'm coming! I'm coming!
BEATRICE:	I'm a fountain!
DANTE:	What a great fuck!
BEATRICE:	I love you! Let's get married!

Telling Them Off: Nobody but Nobody Fucks Around with Me!

Ideally, obscenities are best left unarticulated. But they have a way of bubbling up from tortured depths and straining

Merda!

to the surface like incredibly assertive explosives that perplex even their very own creators. They tend to ferment in the darker regions of the psyche and are part of that internecine struggle between id and ego, anima and persona. They are the strangled perorations of shackled Kafkaesque protagonists whose faces, like green fried eggs, are the visages in the quiet nightmares of Edvard Munch. Wow! As my grandfather used to say, get them out before they kill you. (He had flatulence in mind.) And Italians do get them out. Now and then we must exorcise the poisons. Try it when you're alone. Be wicked! Be adventurous! Be ready for combat! But also be ready for the bluenoses. Their icy hauteur can freeze the redness in our ventricles.

Let's face it—there are times when we have to vent our anger. Things and people do have a way of closing in on us. A shrink is expensive. These verbal blasts cost you nothing more than what you paid for *Merda!*

Fuck yourself! (repetitive, I know, but that is the heart of the learning process)	**Vaffanculo!**
I'm nobody's fucking fool!	**Non sono il fesso di nessuno!**
Nobody fucks me up the ass!	**Nessuno me lo ficca in culo!**
I don't kiss ass!	**Non lecco culo!**
Eat my cock (pussy)!	**Mangiamelo!**
I'm not a piece of shit!	**Non sono un stronzo!**
You're so full of shit!	**Sei pieno di merda!**

You're not giving me the shaft!	**Non me lo fai!**
Suck this!	**Succhiamelo!**
Jerk me off!	**Fregamelo!**
I'm not your goddamned pimp!	**Non sono il tuo ruffiano!**
I'm not a whore.	**Non sono una puttana.**
I'm sick of all this shit!	**Sono stanca di questa merda!**
You can all go fuck yourselves!	**Andate tutti a vaffanculo!**
I'm not down and out!	**Non sono un morto di fame!** (literally, I'm not dying of hunger)
I'm not homeless yet!	**Non sono un pezzente!**
What a fucked-up world!	**Mondo cane!** (literally, it's a dog's world)
God—you are one fucking hangman!	**Dio boia!**

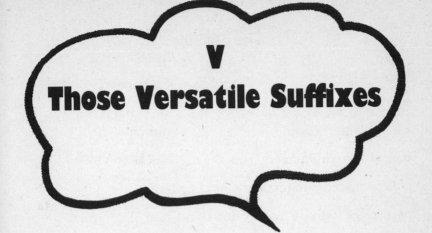

V
Those Versatile Suffixes

How to Make Shit Shittier

In an earlier chapter we tried to suggest the versatility of Italian suffixes, indicating that they can achieve a terseness not as accessible in English. In English, you may find that the one word *shit* is not enough to express your anger at a particular moment. You may have to alter or intensify it with modifiers such as dirty, big, lousy, disgusting, and so forth. The point is that you have to create a cumbersome chain of words. Not so in Italian. The word remains intact while becoming an even greater monster of invective. Note what happened to the word *merda* in the earlier chapter. In Italian, we added a suffix and our scorn became increasingly pejorative or comically offensive. Italian is also superior to its sister Romance languages—French and Spanish—in this suffix flexibility. Without getting too academic about it (editors do lose their patience), let's leer indecently as the already reprehensible grows into something patently objectionable.

The Suffixes

large, terrible	-one
small, agreeable, charming	-ino
small, dainty, diminutive	-etto
bad, disagreeable, repugnant	-accio
a dirty place, a dump, a sty	-aio
permeated with, in a great degree	-oso
very small and charming	-ettino
small, cute, attractive	-uccio
denoting a particular attribute	-uto
an ongoing activity	-ata
to a great degree	-issimo

Measure for Measure for Gentlemen

the penis	il membro
a small penis	un membrolino
a man with a sizable penis	un membroso
a man favorably endowed	un membruto

Merda!

Stronzo and Its Permutations
(All forms of *stronzo* are taboo
and are not to be used casually.)

a big, filthy, foul, repugnant   **un stronzone**
  disgusting, gross, fetid, acrid,
  abject turd or shit

> **Mio marito è un stronzone di prima classe.**
> My husband is a first-class piece of shit.

a small, agreeable, charming shit   **un stronzino**

> **Mia figlia è carina, ma il mio figlio è un stronzino.**
> My daughter is a charmer, but my son is a little turd.

a small shit or turd   **un stronzetto**

> **Mio fidanzato è un stronzetto ricco.**
> My fiancé is a bit of a bastard, but he's got money.

a really disagreeable person, a   **un stronzaccio**
  cosmic shit

> **Vigliacco, non fare lo stronzaccio!**
> Bastard! Don't be such a fucking shit!

a filthy place, a place redolent of   **un stronzaio**
  shit

> **Sono stanco di vivere in questo stronzaio di dodici stanze.**
> I'm sick and tired of living in this twelve-room shithouse!

someone indistinguishable from   **un stronzoso**
  shit

Sei un stronzoso puzzolente!
You are one lousy son-of-a-bitch!

a small, charming shit   **un stronzettino**

Non fare lo stronzettino. Dammi un bacio.
Don't be a little shit. Give me a kiss.

a bad but irresistible shit   **un stronzuccio**

Sei un stronzuccio, ma ti amo.
You're a little shit, but I love you.

Take any of the words you have learned so far, nouns mainly (and don't forget the Glossary), and notice how they can be transformed by suffixes so that their potency grows and grows.

a harmless jerk	cazzo + uccio	un cazzuccio
an uncouth asshole	cafone + accio	un cafonaccio
a fucked-up dummy	coglione + accio	un coglionaccio
a fatass	culo + one	un culone
an asshole	buco + one	un bucone
a drunkard, a lush	briaco + one	un briacone
a good fuck	chiavare + ata	una chiavata
a real old bitch	befana + accia	una befanaccia
a really satisfying blow job	pompino + etto	un pompinetto
big tits	poppe + one	poppone
a real slut	fica + accia	una ficaccia
a devil, a sleaze, a crook	diavolo + accio	un diavolaccio
a damned fool	cretino + accio	un cretinaccio
one who farts excessively	scureggia + one	un scureggione
a real fool	minchia + one	un minchione

60

Merda!

a gossip, a chatterbox	chiacchierare + one	un chiaccierone
an obtuse person	testa + one	un testone
a compulsive masturbator, a cheat	<u>fregare</u> + one	un <u>fregone</u>
one who spills the beans, a character assassin	bocca + al + one	un boccalone
one who can't stop pissing	<u>piscia</u> + one	un <u>piscione</u>
a slob	porco + one	un porcone
a literal *or* figurative shit	<u>cacare</u> + one	un <u>cacone</u>
one whose nose needs blowing	caccola + one	un caccolone
to be screwed, sodomized, made a fool of	<u>inculare</u> + ata	un <u>inculata</u>
a fat woman	coscie + ona	una cosciona
a sly, sneaky one	furbo + one	un furbone

Now you try it with a few nouns of your choice.

Bravo, Bravissimo! (How to Cheer Your Favorite Performers Grammatically)

Despite the inroads of transsexuality, grammatical gender is still grammatical gender, and, at the risk of sounding pedantic, you simply do not shout *Bravo!* when a lady is taking a solo bow.

Merda!

These Are the Correct Forms

for a man taking a solo bow	**Bravo! Bravissimo!**
for a woman taking a solo bow	**Brava! Bravissima!**
for two or more women taking their bows	**Brave! Bravissime!**
for two or more men taking their bows	**Bravi! Bravissimi!**
for men and women taking their bows together	**Bravi! Bravissimi!**

N.B. If you happen to be particularly dissatisfied with the performers, you can use one of the many offensive words or phrases you have studied to express, sardonically, your disapproval: **Brava poppona! Bravo stronzaccio! Bravi spuderati!**

Practice Time Again

1. "Bravissimo!" gridò la donna felice. "Sei l'unico uomo capace d'avermi fatto venire."
2. Quel cazzuccino si perderà nella mia gran potta.
3. Uominetto mio, perchè arrivi solamente alle mie poppe?
4. Cerco uno ricco e membroso.
5. Brutto coglionaccio, fuori dal mio letto!

1. "Bravissimo!" shouted the happy woman. "You're the first man who's managed to make me come."
2. That little dick's gonna get lost in my big tunnel.
3. Little man, how come you only come up to my tits?
4. I'm looking for a guy who's rich and really hung.
5. Get out of my bed, you fucked-up dummy!

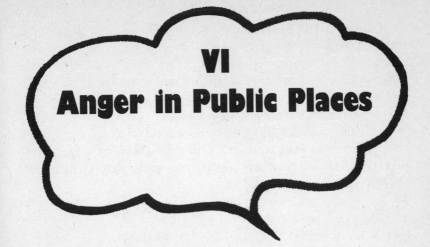

VI
Anger in Public Places

Food and Restaurants and *Supermercati* and *Salumerie*

Italians (let us generalize) are unabashedly sensual. They indulge in food and sex with equal abandon. Ingestion and sex become what they basically are—two forms of penetration. Each culminates in a satiety that placates man's need for love and nourishment. Thus both body and soul are made to recline on the soft pillows of nurturing self-indulgence, and the nervous system purrs like a cat whose whiskers are dripping heavy cream.

Even French pilferage has not relegated Italian culinary genius to the darker corners of gastronomy. Marie de' Medici brought Italian cookery to France, where Gallic duplicity quickly undermined the integrity of good ingredients with unctuous sauces. The French will always confuse egregious decorative effects with creative integrity. They have a genius for appearances. *Trompe l'oeil* will do for a Frenchman, but not for an Italian.

Roland Delicio

If there is still someone we know who has not eaten in a trattoria and doesn't know the difference between pizza and pasta primavera, barolo and brunello, tartufi and tiramisù, bollito misto and balsamella, risotto and spezzatino, tortellini and tortelloni—then be sure to give that person a copy of Marcella Hazan's wonderful cookbook.

Let's take a look at the language of food (we've done it with the language of sex), and let's also take a look at some ways of expressing anger when confronted with poor service and shabby food.

(needs no defining)	pasta
the appetizer	l'antipasto
bread	il pane
butter	il burro
water	l'acqua
the waiter	il cameriere
meat	la carne
vegetables	la verdura
the salad	l'insalata
oil	l'olio
salt and pepper	sale e pepe
cheese	il formaggio
mustard	la mostarda
the dessert	il dolce

Merda!

eggs	**le uova**
the supermarket	**il supermercato**
taxes	**le tasse**
fish	**il pesce**
the steak	**la bistecca**
a glass	**un bicchiere**
tableware	**le posate**
a slice	**una fetta**
a snack	**un spuntino, la merenda**
something to drink	**da bevere**

Use These When You Are Angry with Food and Service

Ma vaffanculo! Ho prenotato due giorni fa!
I made a fucking reservation two days ago.

Questi prezzi fanno schifo!
These prices suck! (Literally, these prices are disgusting!)

A questa tavola ci mangia lei, porcaccio!
Why don't *you* eat at this table, you dirty pig!

Questo ristorante è un merdaio.
This restaurant is a sewer (or shithole).

Voglio un cameriere che non è frocio.
Send me a waiter who isn't a faggot.

Questo vino da niente è un aceto.
This worthless wine might as well be vinegar.

Questa minestra è più sciocca del mio culo.
This soup is about as tasty as my ass.

La carne di una vecchia puttana è più tenera di questa bistecca!
The flesh of an old whore is more tender than this steak!

Merda!

Cretino, ho ordinato l'antipasto caldo, non quello freddo.
Idiot! I ordered the hot appetizer, not the cold one.

Meglio prenderlo in culo che mangiare in questo ristorante fetente.
Better to take it up the ass than to eat in this pigsty.

Quanto? Merda! Troppo!
How much? Shit! Too much!

Questo pane è più duro del mio cazzo.
This bread is harder than my cock.

Il latte d'una troia è più a buon prezzo!
A whore's milk is cheaper than this!

Non ce nulla a buon prezzo in questo merdaio?
Isn't there anything reasonably priced in this shithouse?

Quel zucchino ficcatevelo in culo!
Take that zucchino (the singular of zucchini) and shove it up your ass!

Bucaioli travestiti—non mi fregate!
You transvestite queers aren't screwing me!

Con quella banana, caro signore, si fa un bel pompino.
Take that banana—sir—and give it one good blow job.

Planes, Buses, Trains

The world is a frenetic place. Round and round we go chasing our tails, otherwise wondering when the treadmill stops. We go to where we've been and back and wonder whether we've been there. If you are traveling with children, this book, like certain potentially lethal medications, should be kept out of their reach.

an airplane	un aeroplano, un aero
an airport	un aeroporto
the train	il treno
the main railway station	la stazione centrale
the bus	l'autobus
the bus station	la stazione del autobus
the arrival	l'arrivo
the departure	la partenza
the round trip	l'andata e ritorno
to reserve	prenotare
reserved, taken	occupato
the flight	il volo
the exit	l'uscita
the entrance	l'entrata
the waiting room	la sala d'aspetto
At what time does it leave?	A che ora parte?
At what time does it arrive?	A che ora arriva?

Now we are sick in transit without the *gloria mundi* and urgently in need of an outlet for our irritation. The following might prove useful. The language is ripe and aggressively punishing.

Merda!

Questa è l'ultima volta che Alitalia m'infinocchia!
This is the last time Alitalia gives me the shaft!

Questo aero è un porcaio!
This plane's a sewer!

Quel doganiere è un figlio di puttana!
That customs man is a son of a bitch!

Ma vaffanculo l'Italia e chi la creata!
Fuck Italy and whoever created her!

Quando finisce questo maledetto viaggio stanchevole?
When does this goddamned exhausting trip end?

Il pilota di questo aero sarà briaco o moribondo.
The pilot of this plane is either drunk or half dead.

Scendo alla prossima fermata, cafone.
I get off at the next stop, asshole.

La gente in questo autobus sono tutti ruffiani italiani.
All the passengers on this bus are Italian pimps.

Vaffanculo l'autobus, l'aero, ed anche i treni!
Fuck all buses, planes, and even trains!

Culture: Movies, Music, Bookstores

Culture may be deadly or divine. The humanities may appeal or repel. Will it be rock music or La Scala, Cicciolina or the poetry of Eugenio Montale, Cesare Pavese or Roberto Benigni? You might find these terms useful.

a ticket	**un biglietto**
the movies, the moviehouse	**il cinema**
the film	**la pellicola**

71

the orchestra pit	platea
the balcony	i palchi
the clerk	l'impiegato
a singer	un cantante
Encore!	Bis!
a pocketbook	un libro di tasca
a symphony	una sinfonia
the plucking of strings	pizzicato
slow	adagio
sprightly, happy	allegro
at a good pace	andante
a reigning opera star	una prima donna
a leading tenor	un primo tenore

But even culture is not spared our anger as we continue our furious assaults.

La musica classica se la po mettere in quel posto.
You can take classical music and shove it you know where.

Questa pellicola è una fetenteria merdosa.
This movie's a boring piece of shit.

Vaffanculo! Questi prezzi non li pago!
I'll be fucked if I pay these prices!

Quella non e attrice, è una puttana di strada!
She's not an actress, she's a streetwalker!

Per favore, voglio un dizionario delle parolacce italiane.
May I please have a dictionary of Italian slang.

Merda!

Questo libro mi piace perche è puramente pornografico.
I like this book because it's truly pornographic.

Guarda, signorina, ce lo più grosso di questo libro.
Hey, miss, take a peek. Mine's thicker than this book.

Vado al cinema per farmi una bella fregata nel buio.
I'm going to the movies to jerk off in the dark.

Arturo Toscanini era piccolo, ma che donnaiolo!
Arturo Toscanini was short—but what a cunt man!

Ill violinista ha pizzicato il culo dell'arpista!
The violinist tickled the harpist's ass!

One More Minimonologue to Get It All Together

1. Accanto a quello in un cinema non mi metto. Ha più bracci d'un polpo.
2. Ma vuoi essere verginella alla morte? Dagli un saporetto senza darli tutto.
3. Preferisco la musica classica e un bel libro.
4. Cara mia, io preferisco un bel salame duro e lungo.
5. Sì, scema, così ti troverai con pancia piena e speranze morte.
6. Ma tutte dicono che una chiavata con Antonio è meglio d'un pranzo in ristorante prelibato.
7. Io certe mangiate non le faccio. Mi capisci?
8. Ti capisco bene, cara. Allora è meglio che cammini in vita colla bocca chiusa e le gambe incrociate.

1. I'm not sitting next to that guy in any movie theater. He's got more arms than an octopus.
2. Do you want to be a virgin until the day you die? Don't give him everything. Just give him a taste.
3. I prefer classical music and a good book.

4. Sweetheart, I prefer a long, hard salami.
5. Sure, genius, until the day you find yourself seduced and abandoned.
6. But all the girls are saying that a good fuck with Antonio beats a dinner in a first-class restaurant.
7. There are some things I don't eat. Do you know what I mean?
8. All too well, buddy. Then you'd better make sure you go through life with your mouth closed and your legs crossed.

VII
Let's Keep It Clean

Euphemism

You remember euphemism. A nice way of saying something less nice. Sugar for shit. Fudge for fuck. Darn for damn.

This chapter gives euphemistic alternatives for certain objectionable terms for those of you who are too fastidious or civilized to go slumming in the nefarious underworld of the basically bawdy. The English translations are literal, and you can adapt them to your own colloquial needs.

1. Italian: **Vaffanculo!**
   English: Go fuck yourself!
   Euphemisms: **Va in quel posto!**
   Go to that place!

   Va al inferno!
   Go to hell!

   Va al diavolo!
   Go to the devil!

Va al padre eterno!
Go to the Eternal
Father!

Vaffan Napoli!
Go to Naples!

Va alla miseria!
Go to misery!

2. Italian: **Stronzo! Merda!**

English: Turd! Shit!

Euphemisms: **Antipatico!**
Bore!

Rifiuto!
Garbage! Trash!

Robaccia!
Soiled goods!

Sterco!
Feces!

3. Italian: **Una puttana.**

English: A whore.

Euphemisms: **Una di quelle.**
One of those.

Una poco di buono.
One no better than
she should be.

Fa la vita.
She's living the life.

Una donna di strada.
A woman of the
streets.

Una peccatrice.
A sinner.

4. Italian: **Testa di merda!**

  English: Shithead!

  Euphemisms: **Testa di cavolo!**
Cabbagehead!

Testa dura!
Hardhead!

Testone!
Fathead!

Doddero infelice!
Miserable fool!

5. Italian: **Figlio di puttana!**

  English: Son of a bitch!

  Euphemisms: **Figlio d'un cane!**
Son of a dog!

**Figlio d'una buona
donna!**
Son of a good woman!

Figlio di mamma!
Your mother's son!

Disgraziato!
Miserable one!

Figlio della Madonna!
Son of the Madonna!

Figlio della miseria!
Child of misery!

Figlio d'una madre infame!
Child of an infamous mother!

Figlio del padre eterno!
Child of the Eternal Father!

The Elegant Put-Down

Once again, we would like to provide the more refined citizen out there with the means of expressing displeasure without resorting to the obscene or the ribald. One certainly doesn't want to run the risk of alienating one's friends.

Teenagers nowadays are much looser in language than ever. Adults hardly set a good example. When I was an academic, I prepared several lessons on the art of invective without using the prurient or the salacious. It wasn't easy for the youngsters, but they got the point. One could be insulting without constantly resorting to four-letter words, the domain of those who may not have discovered the infinite variety of standard language.

So, for those of you who do respect the ability of language to be relatively prim and yet incisive, here are some basic Italian locutions that will not ostracize you from genteel society or keep you out of the best salons.

Merda!

You're not funny.	**Non sei spiritoso.**
Don't be a clown.	**Non fare lo scemo.**
Do you know how ignorant you are?	**Sei ignorante, lo sai?**
You're tasteless.	**Come sei sciocco.**
A donkey's more charming.	**Un asino è più simpatico.**
You're really stupid.	**Sei proprio stupido.**
You simpleminded wimp.	**Povero meschino inalfabeto.** (literally, illiterate)
You're really boring me.	**Sei noioso, lo sai.**
Cut out the sweet talk.	**Smettela, bocca di miele.**
Clod!	**Zoccolo!**
Wimp!	**Esoso!**
Creep!	**Zotico!**
Dumb cowboy!	**Cafone rozzo!**
You don't have a shred of finesse.	**Vi manca tutta l'eleganza.**
Your taste is glitzy.	**Hai un gusto cafonesco.**
Moron!	**Maleducato!** (literally, poorly educated)

You lie through your teeth.

Sei uno specchio di bugie. (Literally, you are a mirror of lies.)

It's over between us.

Fra noi tutto è finito.

Nonverbal Slang

One image, we are told, is worth a thousand words. In Italian, one gesture may be worth five thousand words, and most have currency in Italy and where Italians congregate. It may not be likely to see people on the elegant Via Tornabuoni communicating this way, or at board meetings in Milan and

Turin, but where ordinary people come together you might very well see hands, arms, and fingers tracing graceful parabolas in the air. The hands alone have an emotive beauty and are a vibrant accessory to communication. Italian mothers severely scold their children to *non parlare colle mani* (don't talk with your hands), but should we try to suppress what is beautiful and expressive and natural? Is there not a mysterious allure in watching the deaf communicate?

Gestures	*What They Communicate*
1. The right arm is raised and bent upward at the elbow and the right hand forms a fist. The left hand is placed firmly on the upper right arm with force.	Fuck yourself! Go to hell! Up yours! You're not screwing me!
2. The two middle fingers of the right hand are curved toward the palm, making the index finger and the pinky into a pair of tongs.	A gesture to ward off bad luck or an evil spell (malocchio). When placed behind the head, it signals a cuckold nearby.
3. A man cups both hands over his crotch.	I've had enough! You're not doing a job on me! Fuck everything! Eat this! Up yours! Your mother!
4. A man masturbates the index finger of his right hand with his left hand.	This gesture offers a rich variety of indecent possibilities.

5. The thumb and index finger of the right hand are corkscrewed into the right cheek next to the mouth.

If made after sampling something tasty, it indicates an appreciation of the dish. If it is made at a passing woman, it envinces a gustatory desire of another kind.

6. The thumb and index finger of the right hand slowly caress the right earlobe.

This may suggest perplexity, contemplation, consternation, or obtuseness.

7. The index finger of the right hand draws an imaginary line from the left ear across the throat to the right ear.

Fuck with me and I'll cut your throat! This gesture may also signal serious potential danger or someone personally threatening.

8. The nail side of the four fingers of the right hand brushes the neck upward to a point under the chin; repeat the gesture slowly.

I don't give a shit! I couldn't care less! So what! It doesn't faze me! Get lost!

9. The index finger of the right hand is curved and placed between the teeth.

This gesture expresses intense anger, even fury, and is often accompanied by contorted facial expressions and bodily contortions.

10. The tongue slides across the upper lip slowly from left to right.

There is something desirable in sight.

11. The arms are kept straight at the sides and both hands are raised parallel to the ground, the fingers seemingly feeling something.

There is something or someone nearby.

12. The thumbs of both hands are placed in both pockets and the four fingers of each hand open away from the body.

I'm broke! Don't ask me for money! The coffers are empty!

13. The open palms of each hand are raised outwardly and defensively.

I don't know anything about anything! What do you want from me? I'm innocent! I had nothing to do with it!

14. Mouth open, arms limp at the sides with fingers pointed toward the ground, the shoulders hunched upward.

What the fuck can I do about it? It beats me! So what's new?

15. The thumb and index finger of each hand stay open while the remaining three fingers are curled toward the palm. The forearm is bent upward and the thumbs and index fingers are moved clockwise and counterclockwise.

The game's up! It beats me! Nothing doing! Who the hell knows!

A Minidialogue: One person is primly articulate, the other is inarticulate and uses gestures only.

1. **Ti devo dire francamente che sei una testa di cavolo.**
2. (Gesture 1)
3. **Si vede benissimo, asino, che non vieni dal'alta societa.**
4. (Gesture 1)
5. **Peccato che sei un povero figlio d'una buona donna.**
6. (Gesture 8)
7. **Un uomo che parla con le mani è un vero rifiuto.**
8. (Gesture 3)
9. **Non posso più rimanere in compagnia con un maleducato come te.**
10. (Gesture 1 repeated with force)

1. Frankly, I think you've got a vegetable where your head should be.
2. (Gesture 1)
3. A mule like you obviously comes from a lower class.
4. (Gesture 1)
5. What a pity that your mother is a nobody.
6. (Gesture 8)
7. A man who speaks with his hands is trash.
8. (Gesture 3)
9. I really shouldn't be seen with a thug like you.
10. (Gesture 1 repeated with force)

Domesticating the Male
Chauvinist Pig

Men may want to skip this very brief chapter. It is written for women who would like to address the Italian Chauvinist Pig—a creature historically more entrenched than the American—in language unabashedly explicit. Refined ladies and women of a particular sensibility (there may be a handful out there) may also prefer to skip this chapter. We might as well add men of the cloth, nuns, eunuchs, the frigid, the asexual, the aggressively pure, and infants in their bassinets.

First, however, we begin with an introductory mini-dialogue entitled "The Good Old Days When Men Were Men and Women Were Not" in order to justify the indignant barbs that women may want to direct at their favorite gentlemen, which follow the playlet. The Characters: *Il Marito* (the husband), *La Moglie* (the wife). The Time: Not too long ago.

IL MARITO:	Ho fame. Portami da mangiare.
LA MOGLIE:	Si, caro. Pronto.
IL MARITO:	Ho sete. Portami da bevere.
LA MOGLIE:	Si, caro. Subito.
IL MARITO:	Mi prude il culo. Grafiamelo.
LA MOGLIE:	Si, caro sposo. Con molto piacere.
IL MARITO:	Voglio un altra bibita. Portamela senza trastulli.
LA MOGLIE:	Si, carissimo marito. Sono qui per servirti.
IL MARITO:	Andiamo a letto. Ti voglio fregare.
LA MOGLIE:	No, caro sposo. Mi hai fregato per dieci anni con quella puttana della tua amante. Adesso parto con Giovanni. Vaffanculo!
IL MARITO:	Per bacco!

The English Version

THE HUSBAND:	I'm hungry. Bring me something to eat.
THE WIFE:	Yes, dearest. Right away.
THE HUSBAND:	I'm thirsty. Bring me a drink.
THE WIFE:	Yes, dearest. Right away.
THE HUSBAND:	My ass itches. Scratch it for me.
THE WIFE:	Yes, dearest one. Nothing would give me greater pleasure.
THE HUSBAND:	I want a cocktail. And don't dawdle.

Merda!

THE WIFE:	Yes, dearest husband. I'm here to serve you.
THE HUSBAND:	Let's go to bed. I want to masturbate you.
THE WIFE:	No, dearest husband. You've jerked me off for ten years with that whore of a mistress. Now I'm leaving you for Giovanni. So go and fuck yourself!
THE HUSBAND:	Good God!

Yes, ladies, you've come a long way. Let what follows prepare you for any encounter in your lives that might remind you of *Il Marito*.

Non sono la puttana di tua moglie!
I'm not your whore of a wife!

Ritorna quando ce l'hai più grosso.
Come back when you've got a bigger one.

Ha letto con merdosi come te non ci vado.
I don't go to bed with shits like you.

Sono una signora, non una puttana.
I'm a lady, not a whore.

Io gli scelgo, non mi scelgono.
I pick them, they don't pick me.

Non fare l'antipatico.
Don't be a pain in the ass.

Ti manca tutto, scemo.
You just don't make it, dummy.

Non sono una macchina chiavatrice.
I'm not a fucking machine.

Sei proprio da buttare in mare.
You're one fish I'd gladly throw back.

Per amante non cerco un puzzolente come te.
I don't need a sleaze like you for a lover.

Sei cafone a letto e fuori dal letto.
You're a schmuck in and out of bed.

Noi donne siamo finalmente libere delle mutande sporche degl'uomini.
We gals are finally free of men's dirty underwear.

Sono libera della tua carne marcia.
I'm finally free of your putrid body.

Vattene, finocchio.
Get lost, faggot.

Ritorna quando sei un vero uomo.
Come back when you're a real man.

Lasciami stare o chiamo la polizia.
Get lost or I'll call the police.

Vaffanculo, ruffiano.
Fuck off, pimp.

Aiuto, mi da noia un depravato.
Help, this pervert is molesting me.

Non sei il mio tipo.
You're not my type.

Addrizzalo o vattene.
Get it up or get lost.

Scusa, ma non ho chiesto compagnia.
Pardon me, I didn't ask for company.

Cretino, canti una canzone inutile.
You're barking up the wrong tree, buddy.

Merda!

Non sei solamente un antipaticone, in oltre sei un gran coglione.
You're an asshole, as well as a damned fool.

I nani mi divertono nel circolo, non ha letto.
Dwarfs amuse me at the circus, not in bed.

Sono allergica ai ruffiani.
I'm allergic to pimps.

Va a trovarti qualche fessa più ingenua.
Go find yourself a more gullible idiot.

Ciao, bambino.
See you later, baby.

Buona sera, amoretto.
Goodnight, little lover.

Addio!
Good-bye!

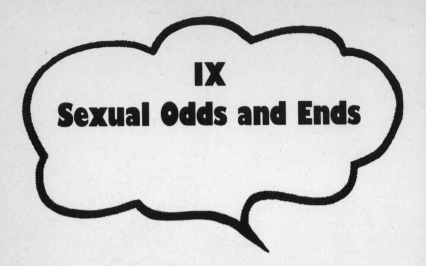

A Penis by Many Other Names

English, from Chaucer to Shakespeare to the present, is not particularly impoverished when it comes to words that are synonyms for the male member. In order to emphasize its pivotal role (comic organ that it is) in the worlds of biology, romance, the erotic, the unseemly, the linguistically varied, and often the simply irreverent, the penis has been compared to a number of objects natural and unnatural. It is a shaft. It is a dong. It is a yard. It is a sausage. It is a boner, a dick, a log, a peter. It is many things. It is doubtful, however, if English has as varied and unusual a list of popular synonyms for the penis as does Italian. In his pioneering work, *Le Parolacce* (Siena, 1991), the Italian author A. Bruttini lists over one hundred such words. Space permits the inclusion of only a few of them.

the anchovy   l'acciuga

the device   l'apparecchio

the asparagus	**l'asparagio**
the big kid	**il bambinone**
the cookie	**il biscotto**
the telescope	**il cannocchiale**
the pendulum	**il ciondolo**
the handle	**la manovella**
the hanging vine	**la pannocchia**
the large pea pod	**il pisellone**
the big bird	**l'uccellone**

Have You Met Miss Vulva?

Historically, we are presently reminded, the role of women has been a passive one. Only the twentieth century is actively correcting this imbalance. Man has traditionally been the aggressor, the leader, the warrior, and the corpse. Women were domestic decor and mothers. They served their men in all respects and, ironically, they too were corpses after succumbing to the punishment of cyclical childbearing. They were hard times indeed.

For this reason there seem to be fewer popular slang terms for the female genitalia. And since the male was the trained aggressor, many of the terms for the penis are derived from the bellicose and from military hardware. Slang terms for the pudenda suggest a receptacle for some of that hardware.

the hole	**la buca**
the crack	**il cretto**

the opening	**il fesso**
the castenet	**la gnaccera**
the large bag	**la sporta**
the stove	**la stufa**
the keyhole	**la toppa**

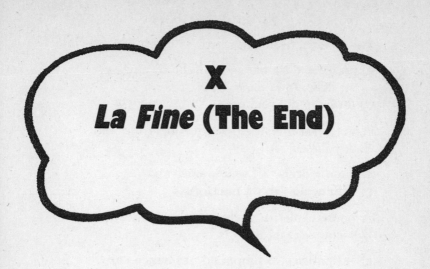

X
La Fine (The End)

Putting You to the Test

The test for a combat-ready army is war. What follows will not be as destructive, but these two short tests will serve to gauge your ability to enter the fray of Italian colloquial slang give-and-take. Propriety may keep you a reluctant listener who still would rather not fire back at those caustic obscenities hurled by the enemy. *Ciascuno al suo gusto!* But if you do fairly well on what follows, it will more or less tell you what you have learned and what you are capable of with some further study. If knowledge is not a weapon, then what is its use? Verbal bellicosity is certainly safer than exploding projectiles on a battlefield, and it has been known to be almost as effective. *Avanti e coraggio.*

Multiple Choice

Place the letter of the correct answer in the space provided.

1. An acceptable Italian word for a son of a bitch is

   a) **un figlio d'Italia**   b) **un figlio di puttana**
   c) **un figlio americano**
   d) **un figlio del regimento** _____

2. A universal Italian taboo equivalent for "Go fuck yourself" is

   a) **buon giorno**   b) **sono americano**
   c) **vaffanculo**   d) **un membroso** _____

3. A polite expletive to describe someone who is boring you to death is

   a) **antipatico**   b) **simpatico**   c) **amico caro**
   d) **soave fanciullo** _____

4. The word whose added suffix makes it even more pejorative is

   a) **cazzone**   b) **stupido**   c) **bravo**
   d) **amore** _____

5. All of the following are Italian slang terms for the male genitalia except

   a) **il ciondolo**   b) **il cazzo**   c) **la donna**
   d) **il coglione** _____

6. A definitive way of putting an uncouth person in his place is to call him

   a) **un fratello**   b) **un cafone**   c) **un turista**
   d) **un bravo americano** _____

7. A polite euphemism for whore is

   a) **una tiramisù**   b) **una signorina gentile**
   c) **una grande bellezza**   d) **una donna
   di strada** _____

Merda!

8. The Italian word for a pimp is

   a) **un ruffiano**   b) **un mafioso**
   c) **un birbante**   d) **un nemico della patria**   _____

9. The Italian slang term for a male homosexual (which, coincidentally, also means fennel) is

   a) **un cocomero**   b) **un melone**
   c) **un finocchio**   d) **un ravanello**   _____

10. A person who has just polluted the air around him by breaking wind has just emitted

    a) **un dolce odore**   b) **una frutta**
    c) **una scureggia**   d) **un aria amorosa**   _____

Matching

1. **la fica**   shit   _____

2. **la minchia**   to fuck   _____

3. **una troia**   the tits   _____

4. **la merda**   the ass   _____

5. **uno stronzo**   the cunt   _____

6. **chiavare**   a beggar   _____

7. **un pompino**   a turd   _____

8. **un pezzente**   the prick   _____

9. **il culo**   a whore   _____

10. **le poppe**   a blow job   _____

97

XI
At Your Fingertips
—A Convenient Glossary

Do you want the Italian slang equivalent of a word or phrase in a hurry? Here is a quick ready reference at your fingertips. The English terms—most often slang and taboo—are on the left, the Italian—also most often slang—on the right. Underlined words throughout *Merda!* are taboo words of various degrees and should be considered as such.

an ugly kid (literally, an abortion)	**un aborto**
an alcoholic, a drunkard	**un briacone**
to apple polish (literally, <u>to kiss ass</u>)	**<u>leccare culo</u>**
an arrogant person	**un sfacciato, un impudente**
<u>the ass</u>	**<u>il culo</u>, l'ano, il sedere, <u>le chiappe</u>, <u>le mele</u>**

Merda!

a bite on the ass	un morso sul culo
an ass face	una faccia di culo
an asshole	uno scemo, un cretino, un doddero, un infelice, un disgraziato, un mamalucco, un buco di culo
an asskisser	un leccaculo, un leccamele, un leccapiedi
a pain in the ass	un antipatico, un esoso, un rompacoglioni
to have an attitude	aver buco, aver culo
an auntie (an effeminate man)	un finocchino, un fichino
a babe (a sexy woman)	una bimba
a bachelor girl (a spinster, an old bag)	una zitellona, una bisbetica
back off!	smettalo! vaffanculo!
to bad mouth	smerdare
a bald man	un pelato, un stempiato
a ballbuster	un rompacoglioni, un rompa palle

the balls	i coglioni, le palle, i testicoli, i fagioli
to break one's balls	bacare i coglioni
to bang, to ball	chiavare, trombare, copulare, far l'amore, praticare il coito
barf, to barf	rutto, ruttare
a bastard	un bastardo, un figlio di puttana
a battle-ax	una vecchia strega
the belly, a big-bellied person	il buzzo, un buzzone
a big-assed person	un culone, una culona, un culaccio
a big wheel	un pezzo grosso
birdbrained	stonato, stonata
an old bitch	una befana
a vicious bitch	una brutta, una dispettosa, una schifosa, una strega
to bleed (extort)	succhiare sangue
a blow job	un pompino, fellatio, coito orale
a bonehead	un testone, un cretino, un infelice

Merda!

a boot in the ass	un calcio in culo
a boozer	un briacone
boring!	che barba! che noia! che giramento!
to be extremely annoyed	girare i coglioni, girare le palle
the breasts	i petti, le poppe, le cioccie
a broad	una bella fica
to brown-nose	leccare culo
bug off! butt out! buzz off!	vaffanculo!
bullshit!	merda!
a bum (a vagrant)	un pezzente, un straccione
to butter up	leccare culo
the buttocks	le mele, le natiche
a cabbagehead	una testa di cavolo
a call girl	una prostituta, una puttana
one who is castrated	un castrato, un gallo, un impotente
a cathouse	un bordello, una casa di tolleranza
chicken shit	merdume

a chum, a pal	un compagno, un amico
an illiterate clod	un analfabeta, un ignorante, un cafone
a clown	un burattino, un buffone
the cock	il cazzo, il coglione, la minchia, il fratello
a cocksucker	un pompinaio, un succhiatore, un leccacazzi, un gustafave
a cock tease	una puttanella
come (ejaculatory fluid)	sperma, brodo, sborra
to come (orgasm)	venire, eiaculare, sbrodare
a con game	un gioco da ladri
cool it!	smettalo!
a cop	un sbirro
crap	merda
to crap out, to be scared shitless	cacarsi a dosso (lit. to shit in one's pants)
a creep	un antipatico
a crud	un sporcaccione

Merda!

a cuckold	un cornuto, un beccaccia
the cunt	la vulva, la fica, la farfalla, la gnacchera, la natura, la toppa
cunnilingus	fare un pompino, leccare la fica
to curse	bestemmiare, tirare moccoli
cut it out!	smettala!
a devil	un diavolo, un demonio, un crudele
a degenerate	un depravato, un degenerato, un scostumato, un pervertito, un sudicio, un lurido, un vizioso
the dick (penis)	il cazzo, il coglione, la minchia
to die unrequited	crepare, morire di crepacuore
a dingbat	uno strullo, una strulla, uno stonato, una stonata
dirt	sporcizia

dirty	**lordo, lorda, sudicio, sudicia**
a dirty deal	**una porcata**
<u>a dirty bastard</u>	<u>**un bastardo lurido**</u>
a dope	**un cretino, un idiota**
a drooler	**un bavoso**
a drunkard	**un briacone, un ubriaco**
damn! damn it!	**maledizione!**
a damned one	**un maledetto**
drop dead (of cancer)!	**ti venisse un canchero!**
the face	**la faccia, <u>il muso</u>, il viso**
an easy make (sexual)	<u>**una fica pronta**</u>
a fag, a faggot, a fairy	**<u>un</u> finocchio, <u>un culattino</u>, <u>un pederasta</u>, <u>un bucone</u>, <u>un frocio</u>**
the fanny	**<u>il culo</u>, il sedere, <u>le mele</u>**
a fathead	**un somaro, un ignorante, un testone, <u>una testa di cazzo</u>**
filthy	**sporco**

Merda!

a fart	una scureggia
to lay a fart	fare una scureggia
an old fart	un bacucco, un rimbambito
a wet fart	una scureggia vestita (lit. dressed)
a quiet fart	un soffietto
to stuff one's face	pappare
fartface	faccia di scureggie
an unclean female	una bicocca
sagging flesh	ciccia
the fly (trousers)	la bottega
to fly off the handle	incazzarsi, arrabiarsi, perdere il lume dall'occhi
a fool, a jerk	un bischero, un asino, un minchione, un grullo, un babbuino, un baccala
a foul mouth	una bocca sporca, una boccaccia
a frump	una befana
to fuck	chiavare, trombare, far l'amore, copulare, fottere

to be fucked up	essere fottuto
fuck it! fuck off! fuck you!	vaffanculo! vai in culo!
a fuck-off	un vitellone
to gab	chiaccherare
a gangster	un mafioso, un malvivente, un camorrista
a geek	un degenerato
to go down on (fellatio, cunnilingus)	fare un pompino
a glutton	un pappone, un ingordo
to goose	metterlo in culo
a gutter person	un scugnizzo, un pezzente
a guzzler	un schiccherone
one who is half-assed	un babbeio, un cretino, un doddero
a half-pint (a runt)	una mezza pugnetta
a hardhead	una testa dura, una testa di merda

Merda!

a hayseed	un cafone, un contadino
to give head	chiavare, trombare
a massive heart attack	un coccolone, un colpo, un infarto
hell!	maledizione! caspita! capperi!
go to hell!	va al diavolo! va al inferno!
to be high (on booze)	essere brillo
hogwash!	merda!
the hole! (vulva)	la fica, la potta
Holy God!	Dio Santo!
Holy Mother of God!	Madre della Madonna!
a homosexual	un pervertito, un omosessuale, un finocchio, un culattino
a hoodlum	un malvivente, un mafioso
a hooker	una puttana, una prostituta
horse shit	merda di cavallo
to hump	chiavare, trombare

to get it off (sexual intercourse or masturbation)	chiavare, fregare
an impotent man	un incapace, un rammolito
to jack off (masturbate)	fregare, fare una fregata, fare una sega
a jerk, a jerk-off	un idiota, un cretino, un babbeio
a hand job (masturbation)	una lavorata a mano
the john (toilet)	il gabinetto, il licito
a joke	una barzelletta
to joke	scherzare
a kick in the ass	un calcio in culo
to kick the bucket	crepare
kiss off!	vaffanculo!
to knock up (get with child)	gonfiare, mettere incinta, impregnare
to get laid	fare una chiavata, fare una trombata
a lay (a woman)	una puttana, una troia, una fica
to take a leak	pisciare, fare una pisciata, urinare
a female lover	una ganza

a male lover	un ganzo
a loudmouth, a bigmouth	un becero, un boccalone
love, to make love	amore, far l'amore
a madam (in a brothel)	una madama
to masturbate	fregare, raspare
to masturbate (female)	fare un ditalino (dito, finger)
one who masturbates with two hands	un ambidestro
to make erect	allungare
a motherfucker	uno che va in culo a sua madre
menopausal flushing ("hot flash")	le caldane
naked	gnudo, gnuda
nookie	una fica
the nuts (testicles)	i coglioni, le palle, i testicoli
a pain in the ass	un antipatico
a pansy	un finocchio, un culattino
the pecker (the penis)	il cazzo, la minchia
to pee	fare una pisciata, urinare

to pee in one's pants	pisciarsi adosso
a gullible person	un babbeo, un credulone
a phony	un falso, un imbroglione, un farabutto
a piece of ass	una bella fica, una fica pronta (literally, easy lay)
a piece of shit	un pezzo di merda
a pig	un porco
a pimp	un ruffiano
piss	piscio
to be pissed off	avere il cazzo in aria
to play the fool	fare lo scemo
the prick	il cazzo, la minchia, il coglione, il pistolino, il ciondolo, la fava
the pussy (vulva)	la fica
a queer	un finocchio, un culattino
a quickie (sex)	un chiavata al momento
to ream (sodomize)	metterlo in culo, un inculata

Merda!

a sausage	una salciccia (often the penis)
a scoundrel	un assassino
a screwball, you're crazy!	un pazzo, tu sei pazzo!
to screw	chiavare, trombare, scopare
sex, sexual	sesso, sessuale
sexual intercourse	coito
one sexually insatiable	un animale, un assatanato
to get the shaft	essere infinocchiato
shit	merda, sterco, feci
a shit	uno stronzo, una persona che disgusta
all this shit, all this crap	tutta questa merda
shithead	testa di merda, testa dura
shitface	faccia di merda
a shitmonger	un merdoso
a shithouse	un merdume, un merdaio
a shitty person	un merdaiolo, un sacco di merda

to take a shit	cacare, defecare, andare di corpo, fare la cacca, fare una cacata
to wallow in shit	sguazzare nella merda
a sissy	un finocchino
to sixty-nine	fare un sessantanove
a sleaze	un spuderato, un fettente, un merdaiolo, un farabutto
slime	porcheria
a slob	un sporcaccione
snot	una caccola
a snow job	una presa di culo
to sodomize	inculare, fregare, mettere di mezzo, infilare in culo
sour	acido
sperm	sperme
a stinker	un vigliacco, un puzzolente
to suck (fellatio)	fare un pompino, succhiare la fava
a sucker (fool)	un fesso

Merda!

a swine	un porco, un mascalzone, un birichino
a tart	una puttana, una troia, una meretrice, una poco di buono, una donna di strada
the testicles	l'attributi, i coglioni, i testicoli
a tightwad	un tirato
the thighs	le coscie
the tits	le poppe, le cioccie, le tette, i petti
the toilet	la latrina, il cesso, il licite, il gabinetto
a twat	una fica, una puttana
dirty underwear	le mutande sporche
up one's ass	in culo
a virgin	una vergine
to vomit	vomitare
to wee-wee	fare la pipi
a well-hung man	uno ben armato, uno ben dotato, uno ben fornito

<u>a whore</u>	**<u>una</u> <u>puttana</u>, <u>una</u> <u>troia</u>, <u>una</u> <u>sgualdrina</u>, <u>una</u> <u>bagascia</u>, <u>una</u> scrofa**
<u>a whorish wife</u>	**<u>una</u> <u>moglie</u> <u>puttana</u>**
a wimp	**un fico, un fichino, un ficolesso, un scipito, una sega**
wise guy!	**furbone!**
<u>a fucked-up world!</u>	**mondo cane! <u>mondo</u> <u>boia</u>! mondo infame! mondo putrido!**
<u>zig zig</u> (the sex act)	**<u>far lo zigo zago</u>**